Feeding the Honeybees

I0440123

D.C. Dixon

This is dedicated to my wife Katrina who helped me through all the negative thoughts in my life. I love you always......David

FOREWORD

Many hours have been spent researching how to take care of our honeybees and supplementing their needs to reproduce. We can have the best genetics, the queen of all queens, and still have the hive fail due to a single missing element that we failed to notice was missing from the hive. I do not sponsor any particular pollen mix or sugar substitute from any company that sells this type of product. To do such would create a bias research to sell one over the other. Instead I will take a different approach and show you how by using this type of supplemental feeding can greatly increase your bee's reproductive cycles.

David Dixon

Table of Contents

Pollen and Honey

In the mid-eighties, when I first started working the honeybees with my uncle during those hot summer months during high school. I remember two important things he told me from that time period. First was not to rob too much honey from the bees and second that it took a frame of honey, and a frame of pollen to make a frame of brood. Now years later, those two issues have caused me to stop and think about what they really mean to us as beekeepers.

To the modern beekeeper it comes down to a numbers game that has been played over and over. How many hives does it take to fill a 55 gallon drum with honey? Or a five gallon bucket for the part-time beekeeper?

When you sit and think about these questions, remember that it is a numbers game for the bees also. A weak hive will have a hard time filling that 5 gallon bucket much less a gallon jar. A strong hive can reap you an amazing amount of honey if you play your cards right and help them.

To answer the question about the 55 gallon drum, I have seen my uncle pull from just three hives enough honey to fill it. This is not a typical average yield and I am sure that some are saying no way. But with his queen selection program and many years of breeding his queens it is quite possible. This was also in the golden years of honeybees before the Varro mite and hive beetles and other issues seen today.

Remember without honey and pollen your hives will fail to produce brood which is essential to producing a honey harvest.

Protein and Carbohydrates

The above two mentioned can be broken down to Protein (Pollen) and Carbohydrates (honey) which sustain life in all forms. Both will be covered in detail in the following chapters.

Chapter 1

CARBOHYDRATES

Carbohydrates for a honeybee come from the nectar produced by plants which is a simple sugar known as sucrose and water. Small trace amounts of minerals and vitamins can be found in nectar. This liquid sucrose is brought back to the hive and given to another honeybee which has the responsibility to place it into wax cells. When the honeybee passes nectar to another bee and then into the holding cell, the nectar receives special enzymes from the bee. These enzymes help convert the sucrose to a fructose liquid (Honey) which can be used as food for the brood. The bees have to fan across this to remove excess moisture and reduce it below 20%.

Honey is by far the best food for honeybees, but when the bees fail to produce a surplus store of honey due to weather conditions, Beekeepers have to step in with a similar product to replicate the missing feed. The two options available at this writing is Cane Sugar and High fructose corn syrup.

What is best? Cane Sugar or High Fructose Corn Syrup Feeding

This has been a common question asked at many beekeeping meetings and I have heard many different theories as to what is the best one. When a beekeeper has to resort to using these types of liquid feed they are trying to accomplish several things. One, it is before winter or in winter and the bees are light in weight and need extra feed. Second, the winter is about to be over and a boost is needed to stimulate brood production. Third, a queen breeder is using these to keep the bees alive because there are too many hives for the area to support feeding them with natural honey.

Let us look at the composition of each and how they are made.

Cane Sugar

Cane Sugar comes from long stalks of Sugarcane which is grown throughout tropical parts of the modern world. In raw form, the long segmented stalks are full of a juice with high sugar (Sucrose) content. The stalks of cane are pressed through a mill to extract the juice. The juice is then cooked down to remove the water content and leaves a crystallized form that requires additional steps for refinement.

Raw sugar is usually brown or dark yellow (**do not feed your bees this type of sugar**) and requires another step to refine it to a white color so that we can feed it to the honeybee. These are several chemicals added to the mix to produce cane sugar. Some experts think that the chemicals used in the bleaching process could be harmful.

When fed to honeybees in a sugar/water form either a 1:1(spring) ratio or a 2:1(winter) the bees has to process this sucrose the same way they do with nectar. The bees tend to go through a 1:1 mixture really fast because this stimulates rearing of the young. The 2:1 ratio will add weight to a beehive for storage during a dearth or winter.

High Fructose Corn Syrup

This liquid comes in several different varieties known as HFCS 42, 55, and 90. HFCS-55 is what is recommended for honey bees. This version is commonly used in soda drinks. Yes, your bees will take down soda pop during a dearth but I am sure this is not a good thing for the honeybees.

High Fructose corn syrup derives its name from none other than corn. There are three steps to converting corn to high fructose corn syrup.

1. Corn to Corn Starch

The corn is pulled from the field once it has matured and sent to the granaries. The kernels are stored in a large container and soaked in a weak sulfuric acid to help remove the hard outer shell of the kernel. The kernels are sent to a course grinding mill where the germ is removed intact. The germ is sent to a cooker and then pressed to release the oil. The oil is used in different processes such as cooking oils and making
The pulp left from the germ contains fiber, protein and starch. The fiber will be ground down and will be sent to make feed for animals and humans. The protein and starch are separated and the protein will be used for animal feed also. The starch is sent to the next refining step.

2. Corn Starch to Corn syrup
   Corn starch is converted to syrup by mixing it with hydrochloric acid and then heated. Pressure is added and the longer the solution is held in this stasis the sweeter it will become.

3. Corn Syrup to High Fructose Corn Syrup.

. This type of syrup can be found in many different foods that we consume today. High Fructose has been shown to break down if left in a heated area too long and this can kill your bees. I have tossed out a five gallon bucket of corn syrup because of the discoloration. When in doubt, toss out.

Hydroxymethylfurfural is the termed used for this chemical breakdown. (*LeBlanc, et al*)

By using high fructose corn syrup it comes in a thin liquid form and can be reduced down to a thinner consistency by adding water. This adds more work to the bees because they have to dry it down before it is capped over. To thicken high fructose to add weight to the bees, add it to extra honey that you have lying around.

For those that want additional information that is beyond the scope of this book please search the Internet.

So which is better?

As of this writing I can not say which is better, and I have used both in many different forms. I think it all comes down to cost and I would not leave the High Fructose in a heated building. As with all feed, treat it as food item that you would want to feed to your family. There are many times that I have witnessed other beekeeper keeping sugar and fructose syrup in containers that were disgusting. Mold and dirt floating in the feed jars, remember why let the bees feed their young like this. The time it takes to clean the buckets and jars will pay off in the end. I have noticed over the years that the more hives one has, the tendency is to go with High Fructose corn Syrup.

Feed Stimulates

There are special products on the market to add to liquid feed such as medication for Nosema or to stimulate the bees to take the sugar. I have used several and have noticed a tendency to entice robbing during a dearth period. Many ask how much I use per quart or gallon but I simply follow the label directions. There is no need to over-dose the bees with essential oils or medications. If you do not want to buy the commercial brands a less costly way is to simply add a small amount lemon juice to the mix.

Ask around your bee club associations about what others are using. You will find that the answers are completely different from each other. Some don't use anything; some will mix a small amount of honey to increase the acceptance of the liquid feed. It's your honeybees and you're free to experiment with these fine insects.

Chapter 2

Ways to Feed Liquid Sugar

There are many different ways to feed honeybees and each person will have his own special way to do this. I have witnessed many arguments at the beekeeping clubs about this subject and I truly think that one has to experiment and find his own way of doing things. I have included many of these methods within this chapter.

Entrance Feeder

The entrance feeder has been a very popular item for many years and will remain so for many years to come. This type has been used by commercial to hobbyist. The small holder slides under the bottom box and uses the bottom board as support. The entrance faces into the opening of the hive. I have seen pints to gallon jars used in this type of feeder. Since the feeder sits outside the hive many suggest it leads to robbing. Also these are not good to use in the winter months due to the liquid freezing and the bees can not leave their cluster to feed. Keep the jars and switch over to the top feeder, just remember to place an additional hive body around it and some insulation type material.

I have placed a greater liking to these in the last several years because it is easy to see if the glass jars are empty.

Division Board Feeders

Division Board feeders have gained popularity with many beekeepers throughout the world. The feeder takes up one frame size in a hive and can hold up to a gallon of feed. The walls are lined with ridges to prevent drowning of the bees. The top of the hive has to be removed to gain access to this feeder. This feeder also has several drawbacks such as a hiding spot for the small hive beetle. One has to open a hive to check if the hive needs feed, If left empty inside the hive, the bees will draw wax cells into it.

The older style was a bane of mine and caused many a bee to die. Anyone who has worked bees knows what I am talking about when you crack open a hive to pull a wad of wax and honey out of a open division feeder. Ask around and you will hear the stories of what these types of feeders can do.

There is a newer version of this that has an insert in the top to prevent drowning and the bees from drawing wax in it.

Top Feeder

The top feeder is a good way to feed the bees without disturbing the hive. A quick lift of the cover and you notice the feed being used. Many variations are used but the one with the access located on one side is the best. The one with access in the middle allows the liquid to pool toward the front side slope and waste liquid feed because the bees cannot gain access to it. I have seen many beekeepers try to make these and fail due to leakage; the bee supply companies carry one made from molded plastic and is highly recommended.

Baggy feeders

These are a different way of applying liquid sugar to a hive and this is to me a very different approach. A beekeeper who decides to use this method needs to build or buy a two inch high extender for the top box. If you try to put this baggy on a hive and sit the lid on it, you can imagine what will happen.

Pail Feeders

This requires a hole in the top cover to allow the bee's access to the feed. A plastic bucket to a quart jar can be used for feeding the bees. The feeders can be viewed from a distance to determine if the hive needs feed. During winter time, I like to place a hive body around this type of feeder with a towel to keep the liquid from freezing during winter months. If you do not have the extra boxes then a small wooden box can be created to replicate this effect. Another item needed is a small block to cover over the hole during moving or non-feeding times.

Bulk Feeders

I have seen many variations on this from a 55 gallon drum filled with straw to a five gallon bucket with Styrofoam floaters inside. This is not a good way to feed the honeybees and will create a robbing frenzy unless placed far away from the hives. Remember that not only will your bees feed but any sugar loving insect around will collect your free sugar feed.

Feeding at Night

There comes a time when work, school, family issues or travel will not allow a beekeeper proper time to feed the bees during daylight hours. All the above feeding types will allow you to feed during the night without disturbing the bees a great deal except the division board feeder. If you do feed with a division board feeder here are some helpful tips to feed at night.
1. Know which side your division board feeder resides on. I always placed mine on the left side when standing from the rear.
2. Feed standing from behind the hive, no need to let the bees crawl up your pants leg.

3. Duct tape pant legs before going to feed
4. If you need to use a flash light, color the lens with a red material, the red light does not agitate the bees as bad.

When I worked full time during the winter months, I used the night feeding with division boards until I switched over to placing an empty box over an inner cover and the placing a jar inside the box. This gives feed directly to the cluster and does not freeze up. Remember the division board feeder is further away from the winter cluster and most bees cannot access it.

One particular night of feeding, I pulled into the bee yard and had the truck lights shining down the row of bee hives. This placed a shadow on the opposite side of the hives but enough that I could still see. I proceeded to feed the bees using the jar on top of the inner cover. It had been unusually warm that day and was in the 50's at night. As I pulled the lid off the fourth box, I heard a sound that will freeze a man in his tracks or make him want to run for cover.

The rattles of a rattlesnake is a sound that many southern beekeepers or hunters hate to hear. I usually have on my snake boots while hunting, but never when I feed my bees. I was not sure where to go or what to do at this point because I was not sure where the snake was. I place my hives on cinder blocks so he could have been under the hive I was just opening or under the one beside it.

I took the only option that I knew I had and that was back to the truck. I used the top as a make shift shield as I launched my self backwards. Needless to say, I had nothing in my truck to deal with a mad snake and decided it was not worth trying to run a snake off and getting bit in the process.

I went back out the next day, to see about running the snake off but I never did see it again.

P.S. A hive tool is never long enough to take a snake out.

Chapter 3

Protein

Honeybees derive their protein from pollen the plants and trees that surround them produce. Not all pollen is created equal and may lack the amino acids to sustain and create life. I have had many a beekeeper tell me to look at the pollen frames and if they are full then everything will be good. This is simply not the case with a key building block of the hive.

Say you are located in the southern states and you either are surrounded by corn, or acres of pine trees. Both these plants produce pollen, and yes the bees will collect it, but it is not the best pollen they can have. I am positive that you would rather have your bees pulling in complete pollen for their expansion than one missing specific proteins. By limiting their pollen supply, your bees will still be able to reproduce but not to the level they could. I think that more research needs to be done in this area.

Protein is the building block for producing royal jelly and once stored into the hive it is quickly consumed by the bees to feed their young.

Wait you say, I know the larva is fed royal jelly at the larva stage and then a different mixture to make her into a honeybee. But where do you think the nurse bee gets the royal jelly? From all that rich pollen and honey mixture they have been creating. This is called beebread by many of the honeybee books on the market.

*Note: In huge queen rearing operations that produce your queens, are you getting the best fed queens? Ask if they are using pure honey and pollen. Chances are they are using a stimulant to feed those nurse bees.

Pollen Supplements or Pollen Substitutes?

What is the difference between the two?

A pollen supplement has pollen in its mixture, at what percentage is up to the manufacture when creating it. The supplement has to be radiated to terminate all diseases and other harmful things that can be transmitted from other bees. The pollen found in the supplement probably came from other bee hives that had a pollen collector on it. The important thing to remember is the amino acids present in the pollen. A complete profile of amino acids is what makes it a protein. You can make your own pollen supplements using ingredients from your home apiary.

Example:

1 cup of fresh pollen
1 cup of sugar
1 cup of water

Mix the mixture up to the consistency of peanut butter. You may have to add more water to get the consistency right. I will give you additional tips later on how to use a bag of commercial bought pollen supplements to make your bees love it.

A pollen substitute is just that a substitute, and has no pollen in it. There have been recipes over the years to create this and Brewer's yeast is the main ingredient that comes to mind. The bees can take in a powered form of this by simply pouring an amount into a shoebox and setting it out. The honeybees will find it and dust themselves in it. Remember to bring the extra back in at night because the moisture in the night air will make it a mess. Those that live in the drier regions can leave it out but some critters might try to eat it.

During the spring months in Georgia, I will often open up the big garage doors on the honey house and let the fresh air in while I work on the many projects I have. We have a black cat named Spooky who will often times come out and lounge around in the shop. I got a call one afternoon about a swarm and dropped everything I was doing, grabbed my bee vacuum, tools, latter and smoker and locked the garage up. The trip was 15 miles away and I got there just before the sun was about to set. This was a nice swarm and not high up in a tree like most swarms are.

I shook the swarm off into a swarm box. This is a box that has the bottom already fastened on, and a large screened across the entrance. The top is a normal wooden top with no sides, very similar to a migratory top. The entrance has a hole in it to let the bees come and go until I am ready to move them. I have found over the years that a five frame nuc box is just too small for most swarms in southeast Georgia. The last dozen swarms I have caught would not fit in a five gallon bucket, much less a small nuc box.

After talking with the property owner, I headed back to the house with the new swarm. I placed it near the honey house and went to take a bath. I never went back into the honey hose until late the next day and to my surprise, the cat had been locked up. With the cat hightailing it out the door, I noticed right away that something was wrong.

The pollen powder was all over the honey room floor. The cat decided for some reason that pollen powder was good and had tore open the bag. This was a big 50lb bag of pollen and you can imagine how hard it was to clean up.

Speaking of the incident with the cat named Spooky. When I now receive 50lb bags of pollen supplement I pour it right into five gallon buckets. It will take several of these but it is a good idea to keep the moisture out. It will also keep the wax moth from making a nice meal out of it. Yes, the pollen inside the supplement will attract wax moths to it.

Making the Patty

There are several things that you need before you get your hands dirty here. This is for making a smaller batch of patties. Yields will be different for everyone because when you scoop out the batter, it will depend on how much you scoop out.

1. A large metal mixing bowl.
2. A small metal spatula.
3. A box of wax paper
4. A measuring cup. Larger 2 cup size.
5. Lemon Juice or Bee Healthy
6. Cinnamon
7. Pollen Powder
8. Freezer paper
9. Sugar or High fructose corn syrup

I start off by pulling roughly about twice as many pieces of wax paper off as I have hives. So if you have 10 hives pull off 20 pieces approximately 12 x12 squares. Stack these to the side. Measure out about three scoops of pollen and pour this into the mixing bowl.

Pour 2 cup of water to the mixture, ½ cup of Lemon juice or Bee Healthy, sprinkle cinnamon powder over the top. Stir it up but you will notice that you need more liquid. Add 1 cup of sugar or High Fructose corn syrup to the mix and stir until you get a consistency of peanut butter. To soupy then it will run between the bars and make a mess.

Okay, I know everyone is asking about the cinnamon. The reason that I use cinnamon in the mix is that I have found that the small hive beetle does not care for this. If you live in an area with no hive beetles then just leave it out. The bees can live with out it.

If you have different types of pollen supplement or substitute, you can combine them together.

Storing your Pollen Patties

Once you have finish making the pollen patty, then find a box or small bucket to place it in. A good idea is to take freezer paper and place this in-between each layer. This will keep the pollen patties from sticking together. If you don't have this or have run out then don't worry. The patties can be thawed out and split apart prior to going to the honey yard.

I make sure they are good and thawed out before placing them on the hives. After removing the honey supers off down to the top of the brood chamber, I hold the patty in my left hand and use the hive tool to chop slices into the patty so the bees can get to it better. Right away, you should see bees tearing at the paper and sampling the protein patty.

Chapter 4

When to Feed

This is a good question and probably the hardest to answer. I will cover pollen patties and syrup separately. Both can be fed at the same time of course, but there will be times when you don't need to feed both.

When I was raising queens and packages, I constantly keep feed on the bees. There was no time when the jars ran empty. Remember, you don't have to worry about getting honey and sugar mixed while breeding queens. You will not be extracting the honey from a starter or finisher colony.

Sugar Feed

Use the liquid feed anytime that a colony gets light to boost the hives weight up. Be careful on this, if your hive is in a yard full of other hives and they are bringing in honey or gaining weight, the other bees could be robbing your hive out. This is when you need to move that hive to a separate yard, check for a queen and start feeding. A robbed hive could be the sign of a weak or dead queen. Always check her condition. If you can not get a queen, then combining the hive with a stronger hive is your only option.

I watch the bees for the first sign of pollen gathering in spring, usually around the end of January or first of February in Southeast Georgia. The hives will go to a 1:1 mix ratio to stimulate the brood production. Never switch over until you see this activity on the landing boards because a miss calculation can cause your bees to over populate and starve. We sometimes have a cold snap around Easter time and then the bees are in full force getting their nectar from the plants.

Pollen Feed

The time to feed pollen is also the start of the spring even if they are bringing in small amounts of pollen from the maple trees. I have placed a few pollen traps on a bee hive and monitored year round when the bees are bringing in pollen and when they are not. The trees produce pollen in cycles, but remember the amounts do vary according to the weather.

Ask around at your bee clubs to find out if any one has a rough time scale on when the pollen is coming in. You will be surprised at what information you will find on the internet also. Don't just settle for the old method of "Well, just crack open the hive and see if there is any pollen in there." Chances are it is not enough to keep the colony going.

Looking at a hive next to yours could yield varying results because honeybees will use up their stores differently. I have robbed a comb of pollen to give the hive next to it more pollen. I felt this was only in an emergency and I placed a pollen patty on them both later that day. I have seen hives get pollen blocked, this is when there are frames of pollen or honey blocking the queen from laying and these need to be moved to allow her to expand. If you get too many frames filled with pollen, one can always store them in a freezer for a later date.

Planting for feed

If you have a few hives then planting around the house or in a small garden can result in increasing their feed. The bees will gather food from many plants and having specific plants that yield pollen or nectar through out the year is important. Different locations will yield different types of plants for that area.

An example of this is in the September month in Southeast Georgia, we plant roughly ½ acre of broccoli. I pick the broccoli, well the small amount that I will eat and let the rest go to seed. The broccoli plant will sprout many blooming flowers and the yields of pollen helps the bees. Note, the plants will not give off huge amounts but for the cost of the seed and the ease of planting, I find this plant worth trying out.

In South Georgia, the fall months have Goldenrod all over the ditches, but I have never received any honey from these like I did in Pennsylvania. Through research, I did find a plant that blooms in late fall, and produces fruit in the spring. This plant is the opposite of the apple, orange and other fruit plants. The loquat tree comes from China area, and is very similar to the apple tree. The fruit can be used to make jams and jellies and I have sold jars along side the honey at festivals.

Experiment with different plants and trees to find out what will work for you. I have often gone to nurseries during a dry spell to see what plants the bees are flying around.

For large amounts of hives, I think the best advice is to find land, which has different types of bloom throughout the season. If not, then moving them or supplemental feeding will be the only way to keep the honeybees going. It might be easier to group hives in large clusters only during heavy nectar times, remember that bees will rob out weaker hives if they need feed.

Where to get the feed

I had to add this section to the book, because it is an interesting subject. On the small scale, a beekeeper has to simply go to the grocery store and buy 5 pound bags of sugar. Keeping an eye out for specials and you would be surprised what you can find. Certain stores cashiers might be inquisitive of why you are buying so many bags of sugar. Just explain that you're feeding the honeybees and not brewing anything illegal.

For the larger beekeepers, there was once a time in the past to purchase truckloads of sugar at the refineries. Tons were thrown out if it hit the floor, or did not pass strict requirements. Government regulations restrict this sale, even if you explain it is for honeybees, they will say no and destroy it.

Fifty pound bags can be bought at lower cost from companies, search around or ask other beekeepers at your local associations.

High fructose Corn syrup can be bought from many locations in various sizes. The most popular is in drums or tanker trucks for the commercial beekeepers. Remember just ask around, you will be surprised where beekeepers are getting their supplements.

Conclusion

My intent on writing this book is that I hope to not add confusion but to clarify the many myths behind keeping bees. There are many great writers that have contributed their parts to the bees and I feel that maybe I have added my part. I am sure that with time, the information contained within these pages will change as have the bee keeping industry. As with all facts of life, what you eat is what you are. The honeybees don't require steaks and potatoes, just nectar and pollen. While you can not take the place of Mother Nature, you can help out by stepping in when Mother Nature is having a bad year.

Please follow us on Facebook at Feeding the bees-kickstarter.
https://www.facebook.com/pages/Feeding-the-bees-Kickstarter/679044185543034?ref=aymt_homepage_panel

Twitter
http://www.twitter.com/WriterDCDixon

On Amazon Author

amazon.com/author/dixondavid

https://www.facebook.com/profile.php?id=100008067048376

&fref=nf

David C. Dixon lives in Southeast Georgia with his lovely wife Katrina. In his spare time, he is an avid reptile breeder, still has a few hives of honeybees and loves to write short stories. He has been writing since his teenage years and has several short stories waiting for release.

References

Leblanc, W.; Eggleston, G.; Sammataro, D.; Cornett, C.; Dufault, R.; Deeby, T.; St Cyr, E. (13 July 2009). "Formation of hydroxymethylfurfural in domestic high-fructose corn syrup and its toxicity to the honey bee (Apis mellifera)". Journal of Agricultural and Food Chemistry 57 (16): 7369.